Leah's Art

Leah Angelina Goldsmith

Copyright © 2024 by Leah Angelina Goldsmith. 859838

All rights reserved. No part of this book may be reproduced or transmitted in any form or by any means, electronic or mechanical, including photocopying, recording, or by any information storage and retrieval system, without permission in writing from the copyright owner.

To order additional copies of this book, contact:
Xlibris
844-714-8691
www.Xlibris.com
Orders@Xlibris.com

ISBN: Softcover 979-8-3694-3146-7
Hardcover 979-8-3694-3145-0
EBook 979-8-3694-3144-3

Library of Congress Control Number: 2024921209

Print information available on the last page

Rev. date: 11/08/2024

Table of Contents

1. Jean-Michel Basquiat 1
2. Central Park 2
3. Pablo Picasso 3
4. Self Portrait – Leah Goldsmith 4
5. Frida Kahlo 5
6. Claude Monet 6
7. Wassily Kandinsky 7
8. Chrysler Building 8
9. Brooklyn 9
10. Morris-Jumel Mansion-Museum 10
11. Family Portrait 11
12. Fernando Botero 12
13. Pablo Picasso 13
14. Claude Monet 14
15. Emma Thomas 15
16. Flowers 16

17. Cactus	17
18. Georgia O'Keefe	18
19. Pablo Picasso	19
20. Maya Angelou	20
21. New York City, Statue of Liberty	21
22. George Washington Bridge	22
23. Wassily Kandinsky	23
24. Keith Harring	24
About the Author	25

Leah's Art

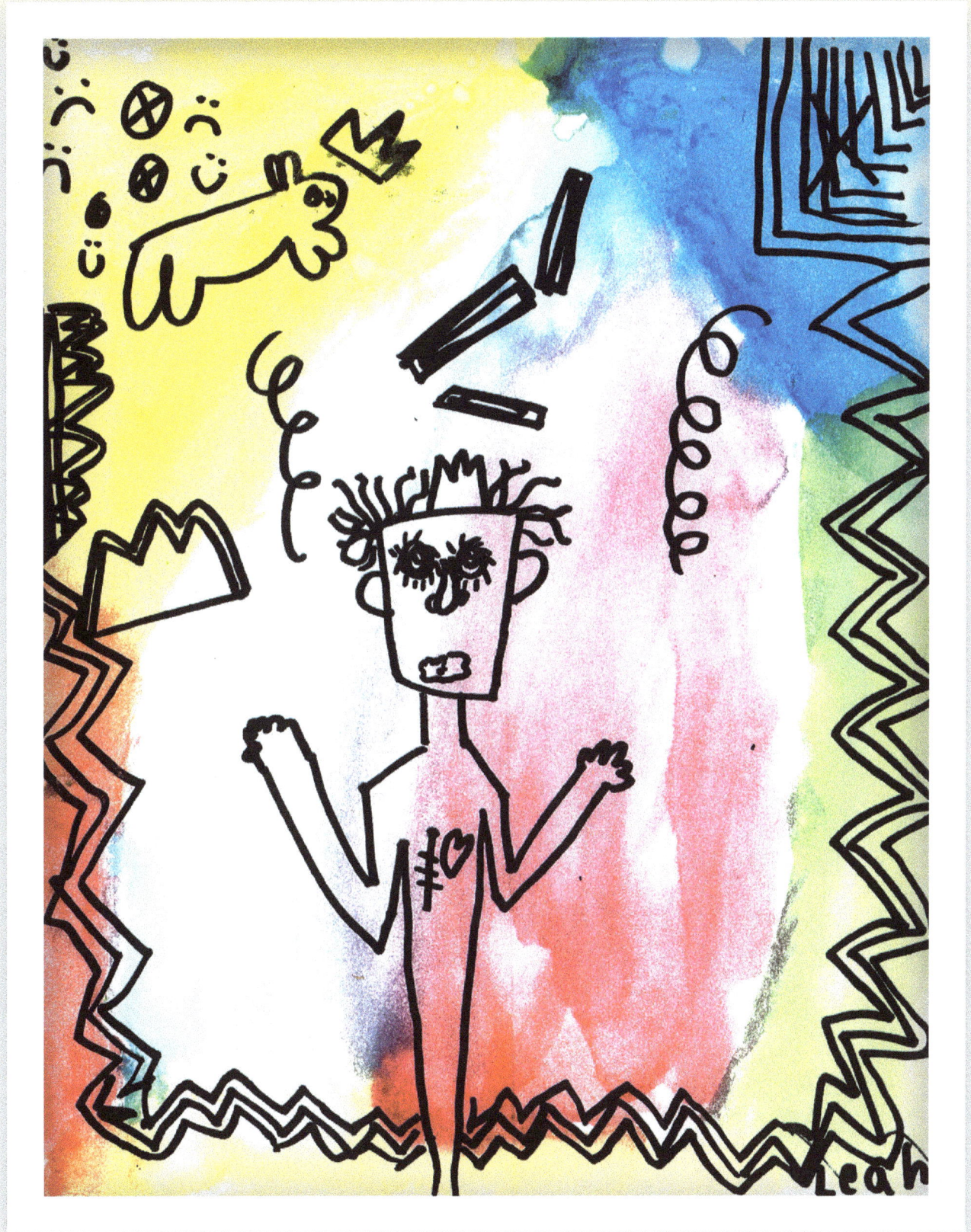

Jean-Michel Basquiat

1

Leah Angelina Goldsmith

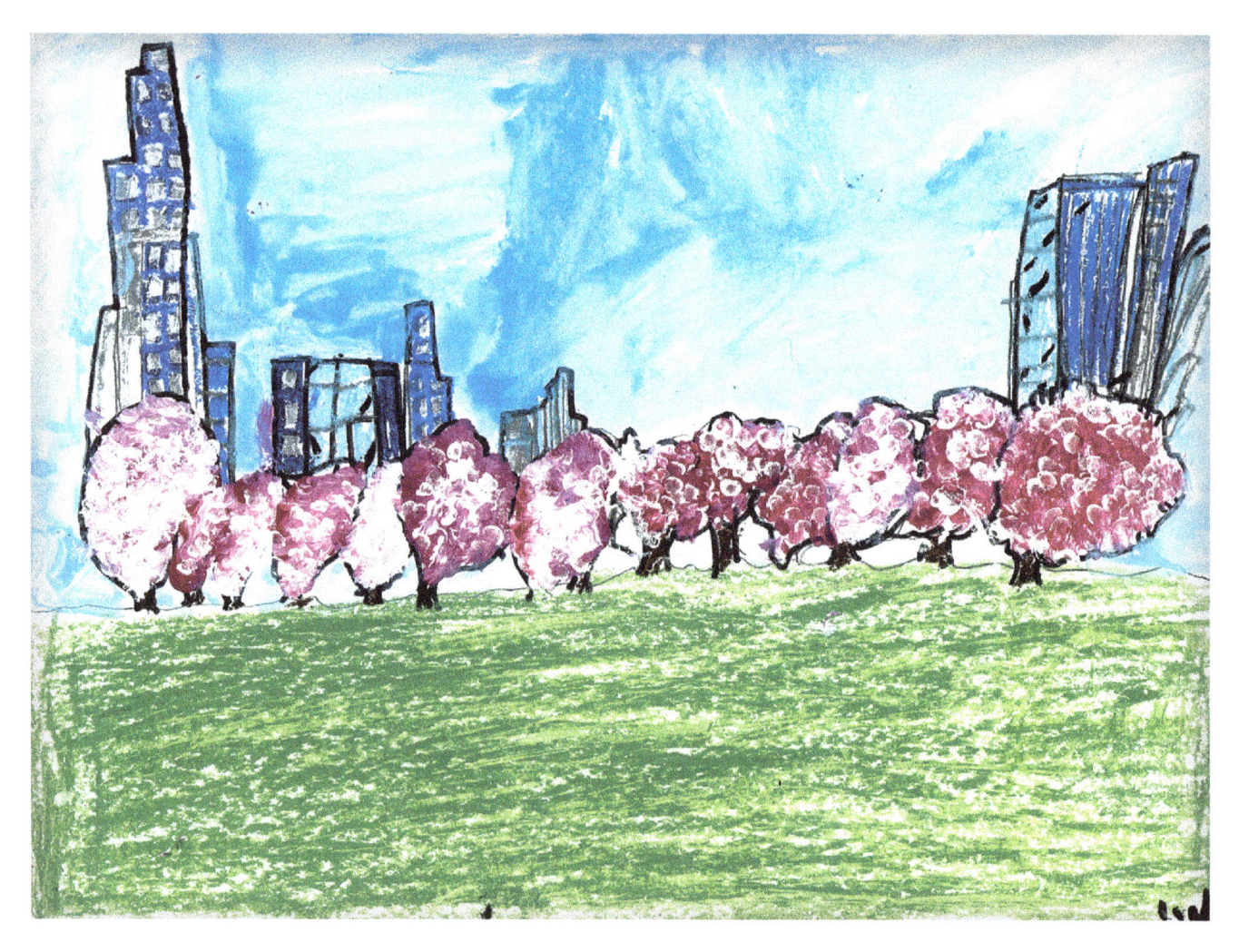

Central Park

Leah's Art

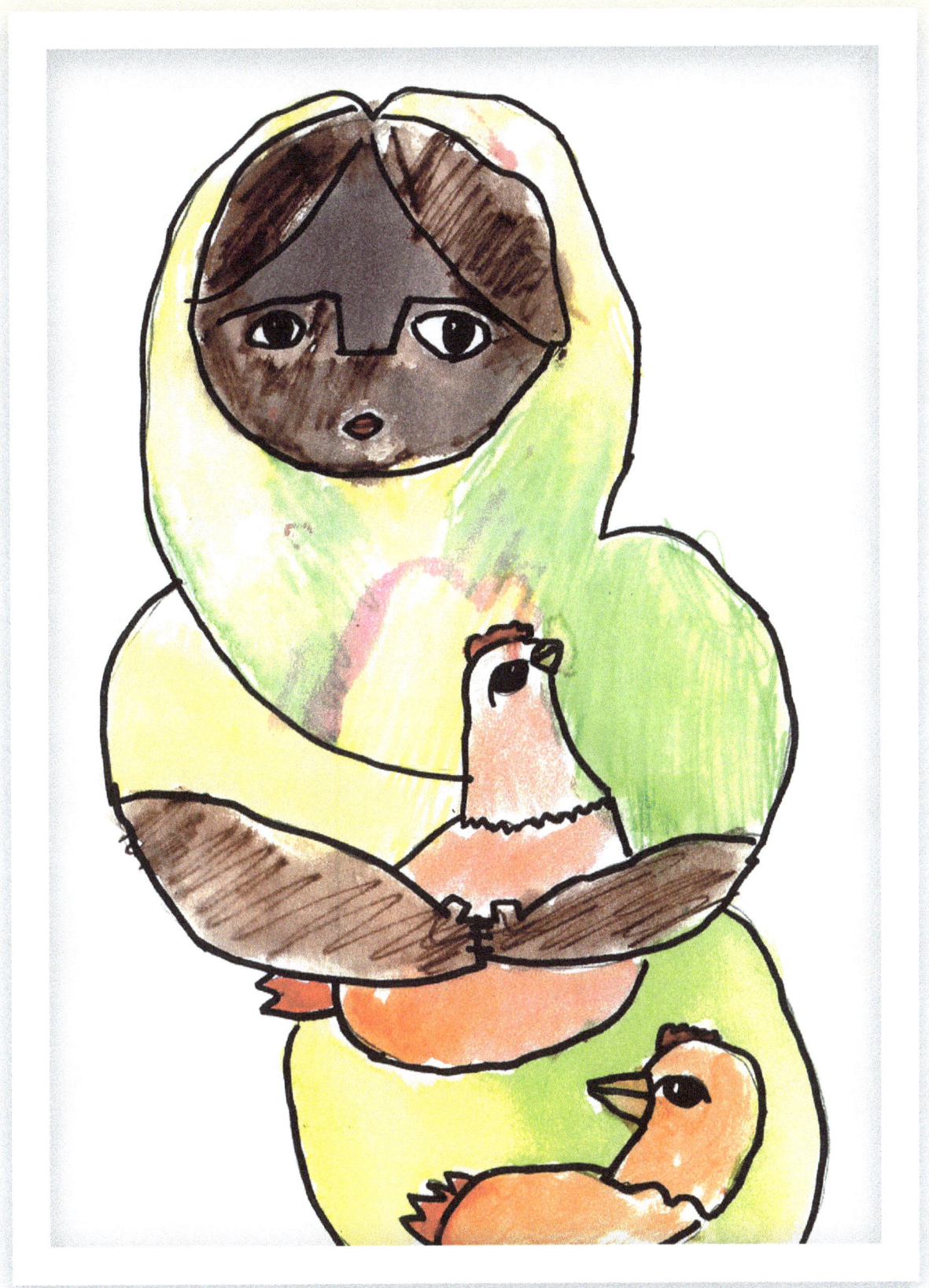

Pablo Picasso

Leah Angelina Goldsmith

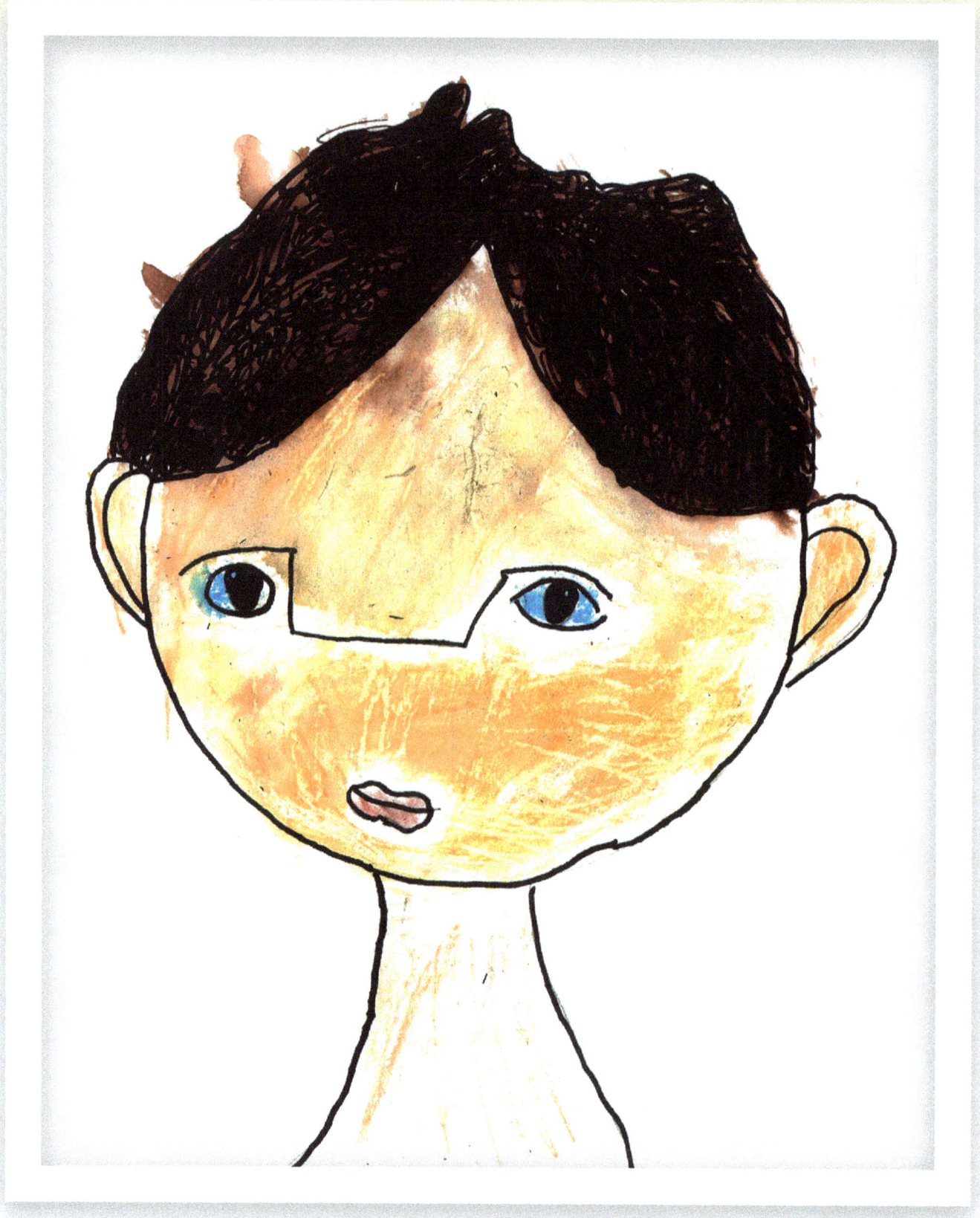

Self Portrait – Leah Goldsmith

Leah's Art

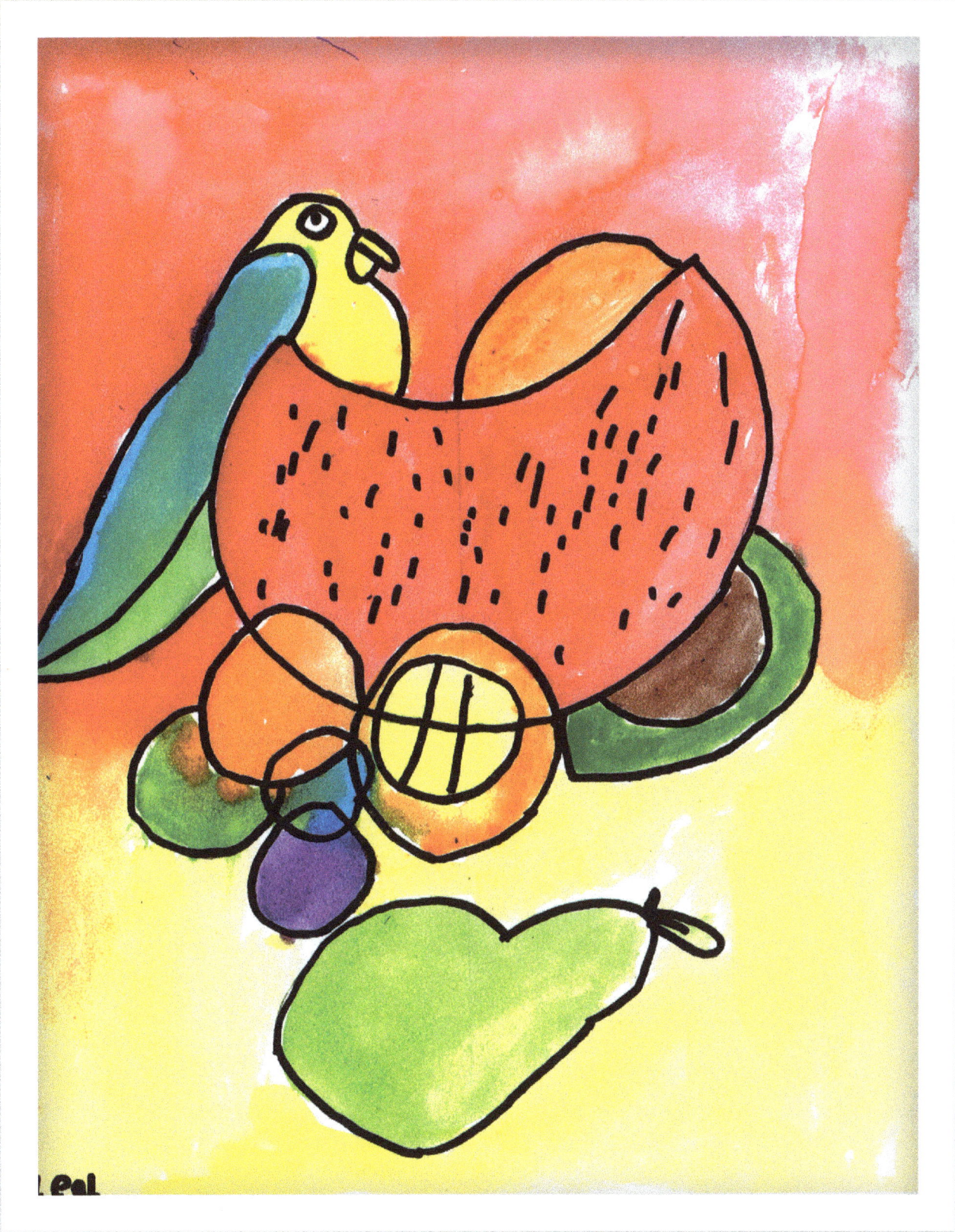

Frida Kahlo

Leah Angelina Goldsmith

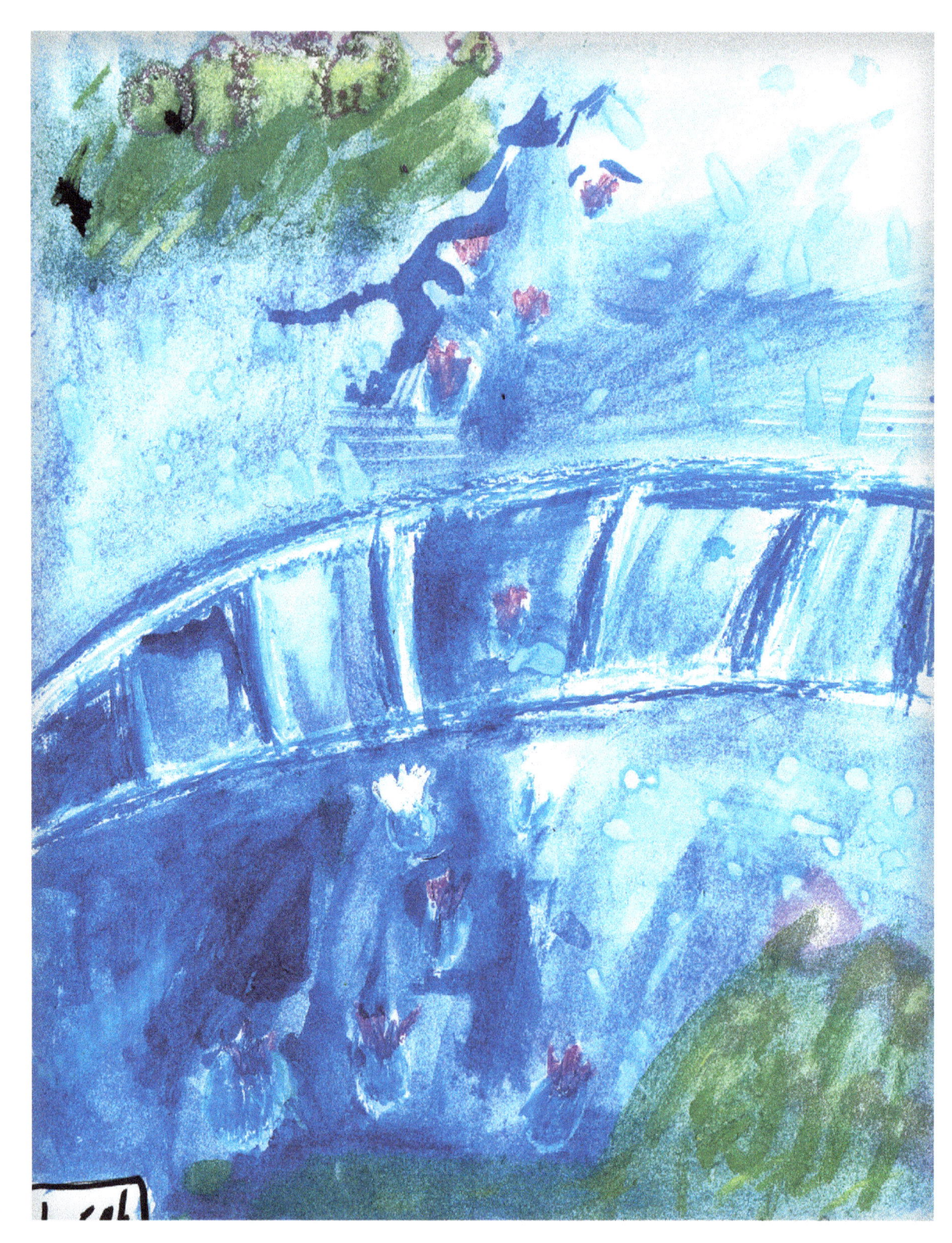

Claude Monet

Leah's Art

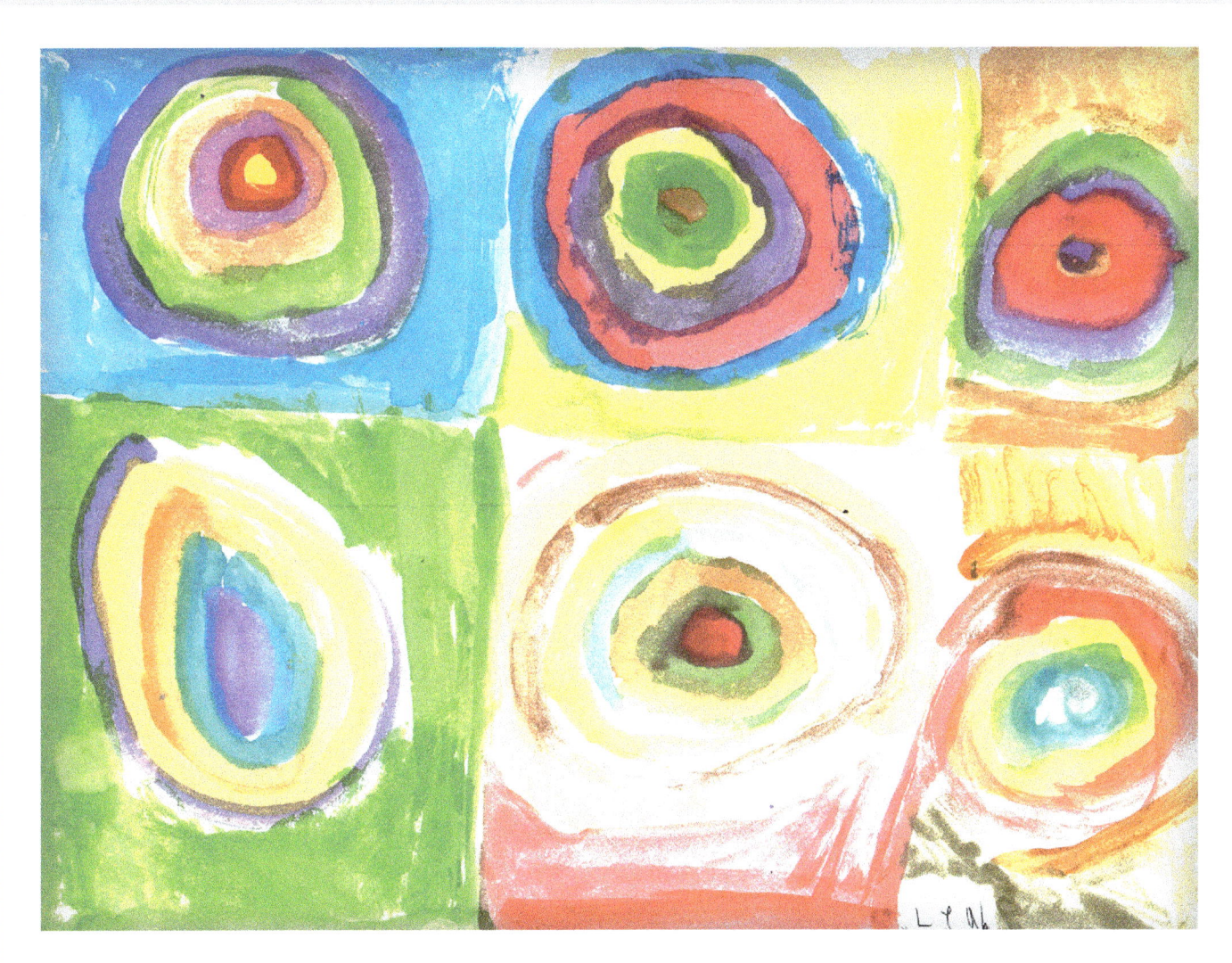

Wassily Kandinsky

Leah Angelina Goldsmith

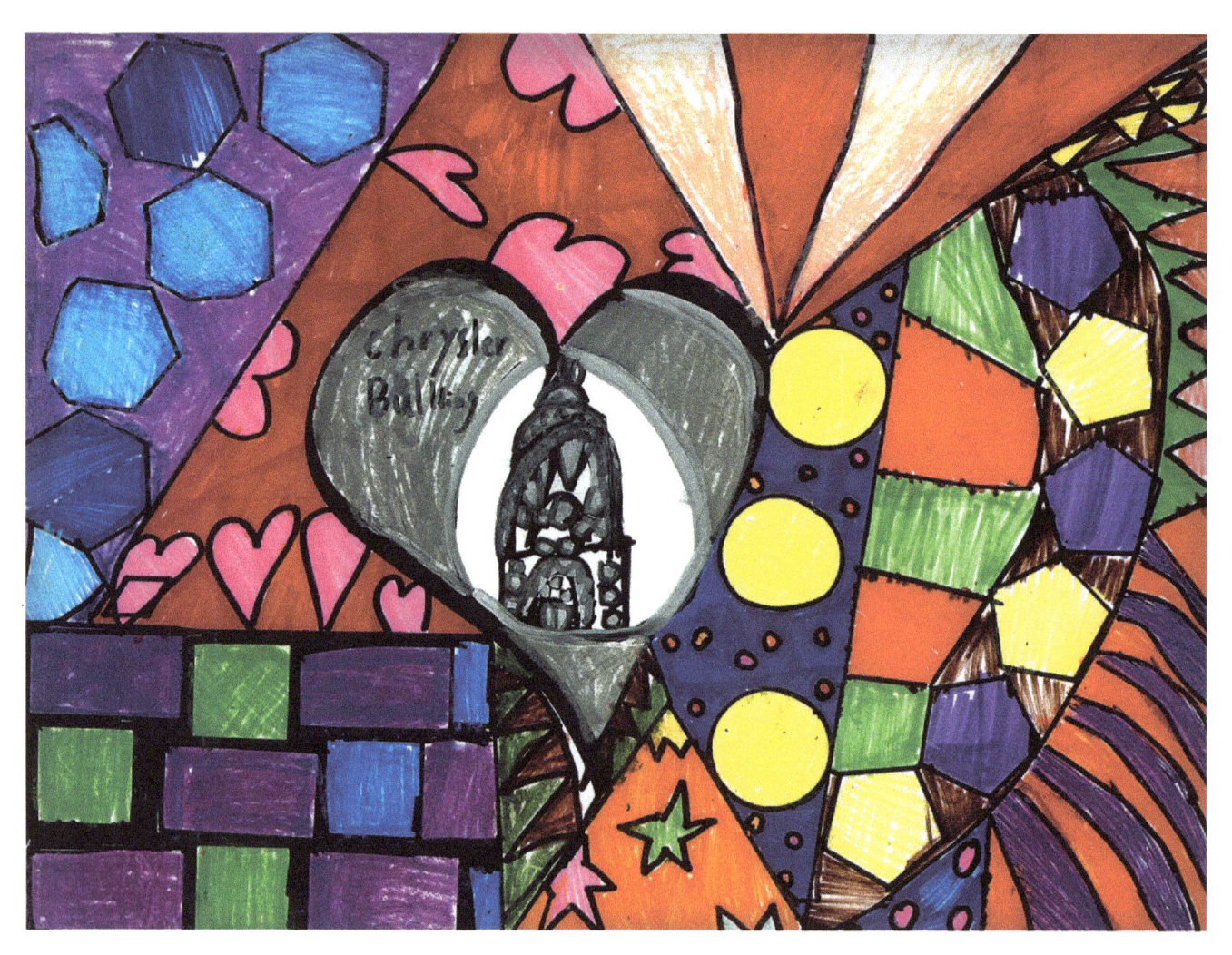

Chrysler Building

Leah's Art

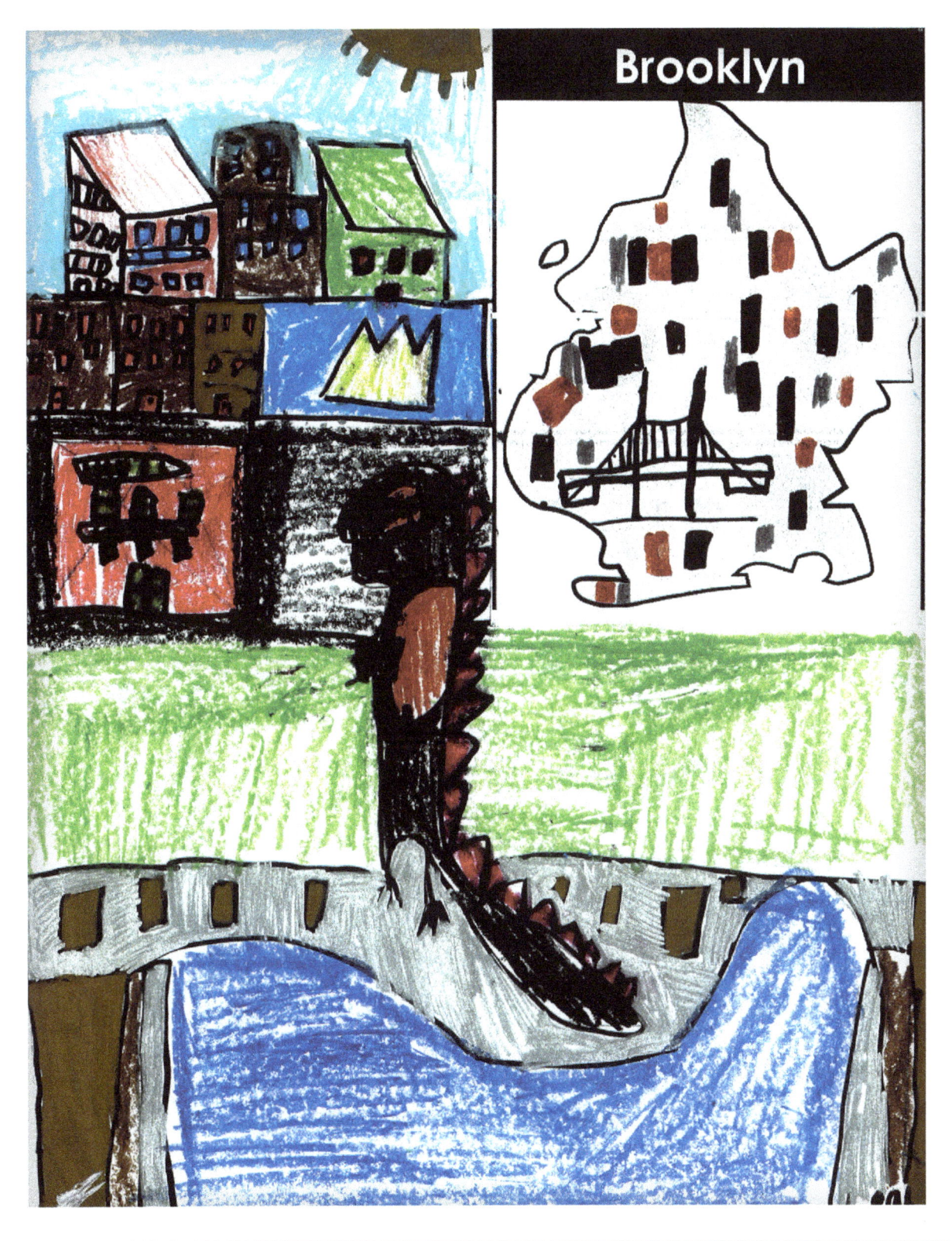

Brooklyn

Leah Angelina Goldsmith

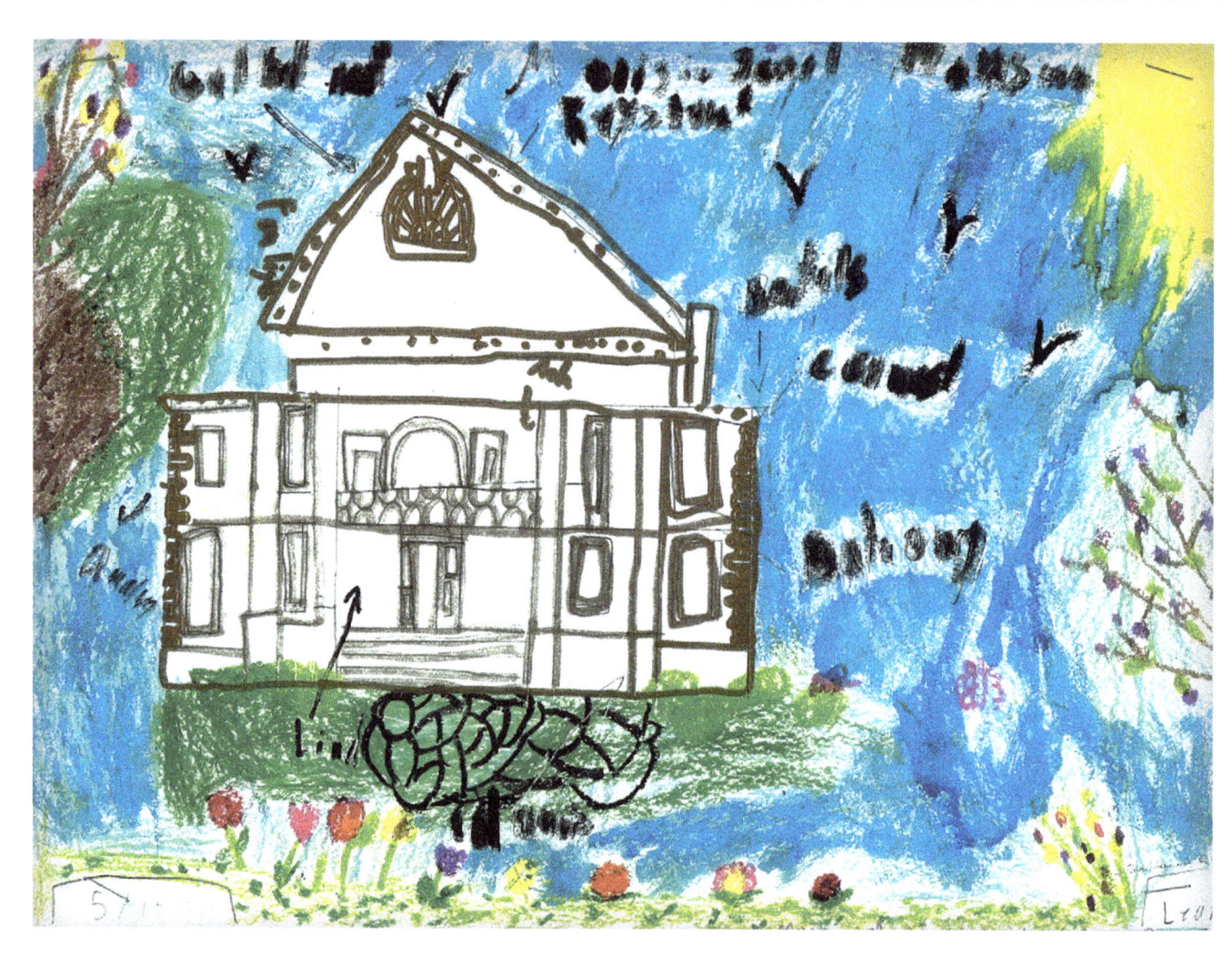

Morris-Jumel Mansion-Museum

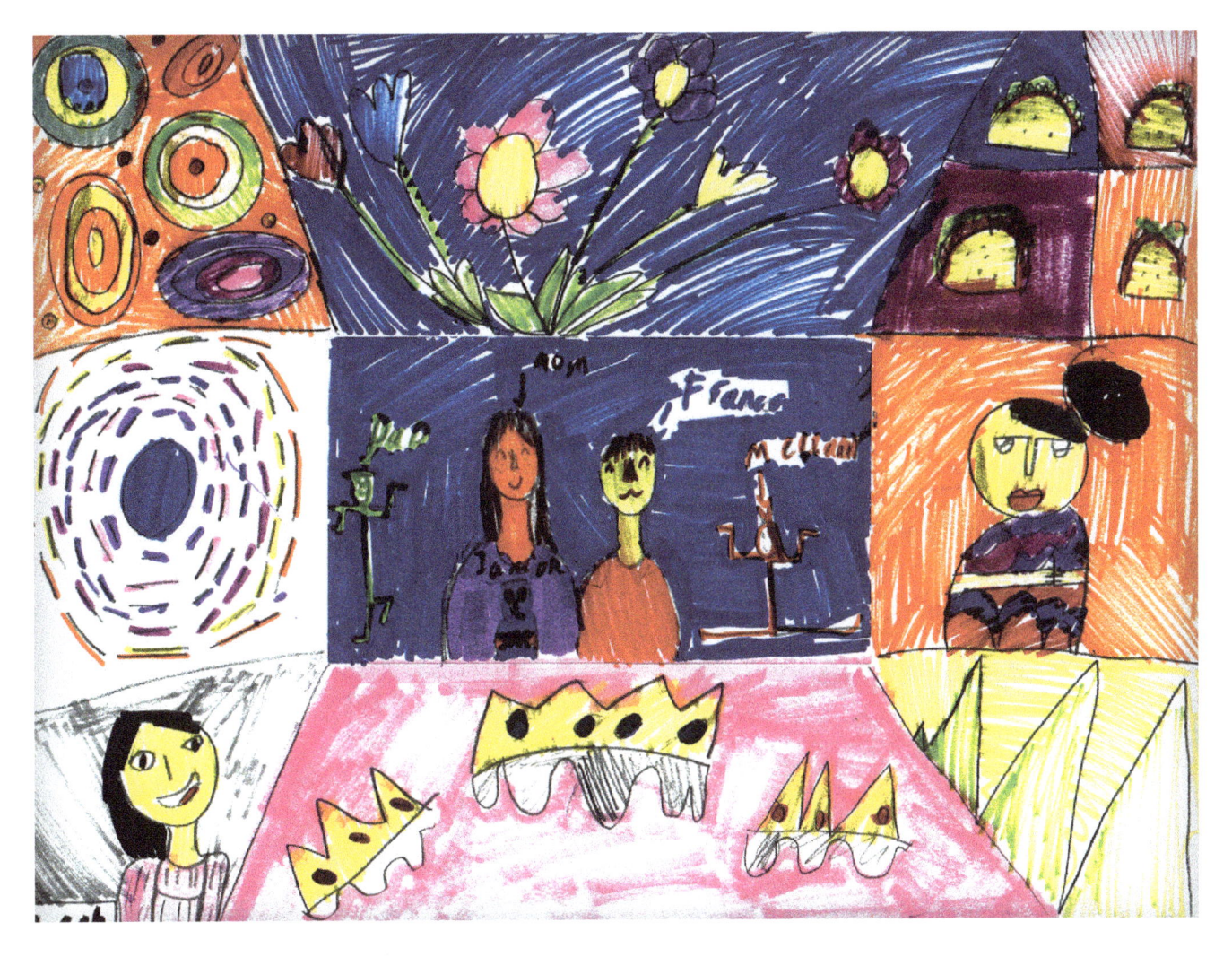

Family Portrait

Dad Howard, Brother Franco, Leah, Mom Rosanna

Leah Angelina Goldsmith

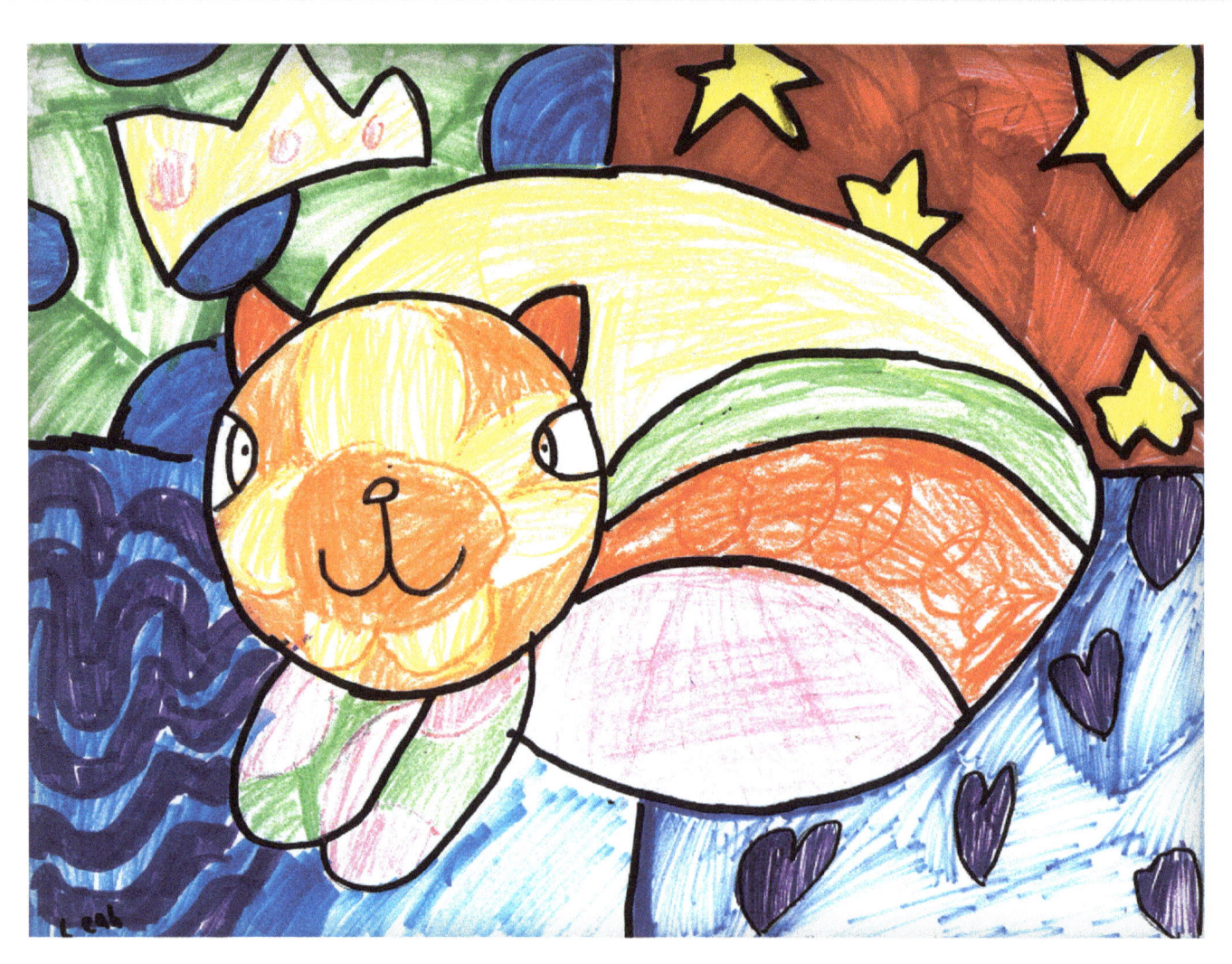

Fernando Botero

Leah's Art

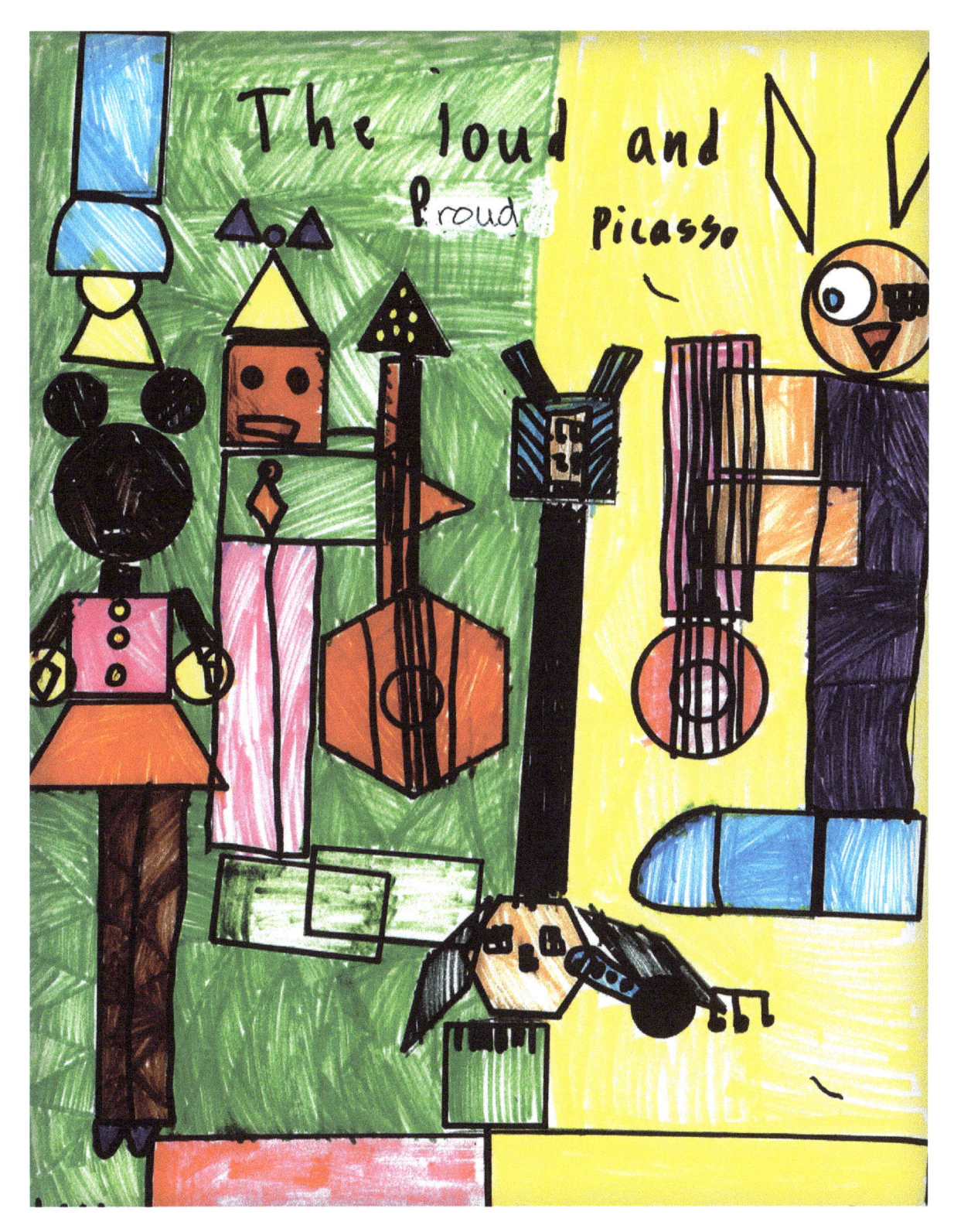

Pablo Picasso

Leah Angelina Goldsmith

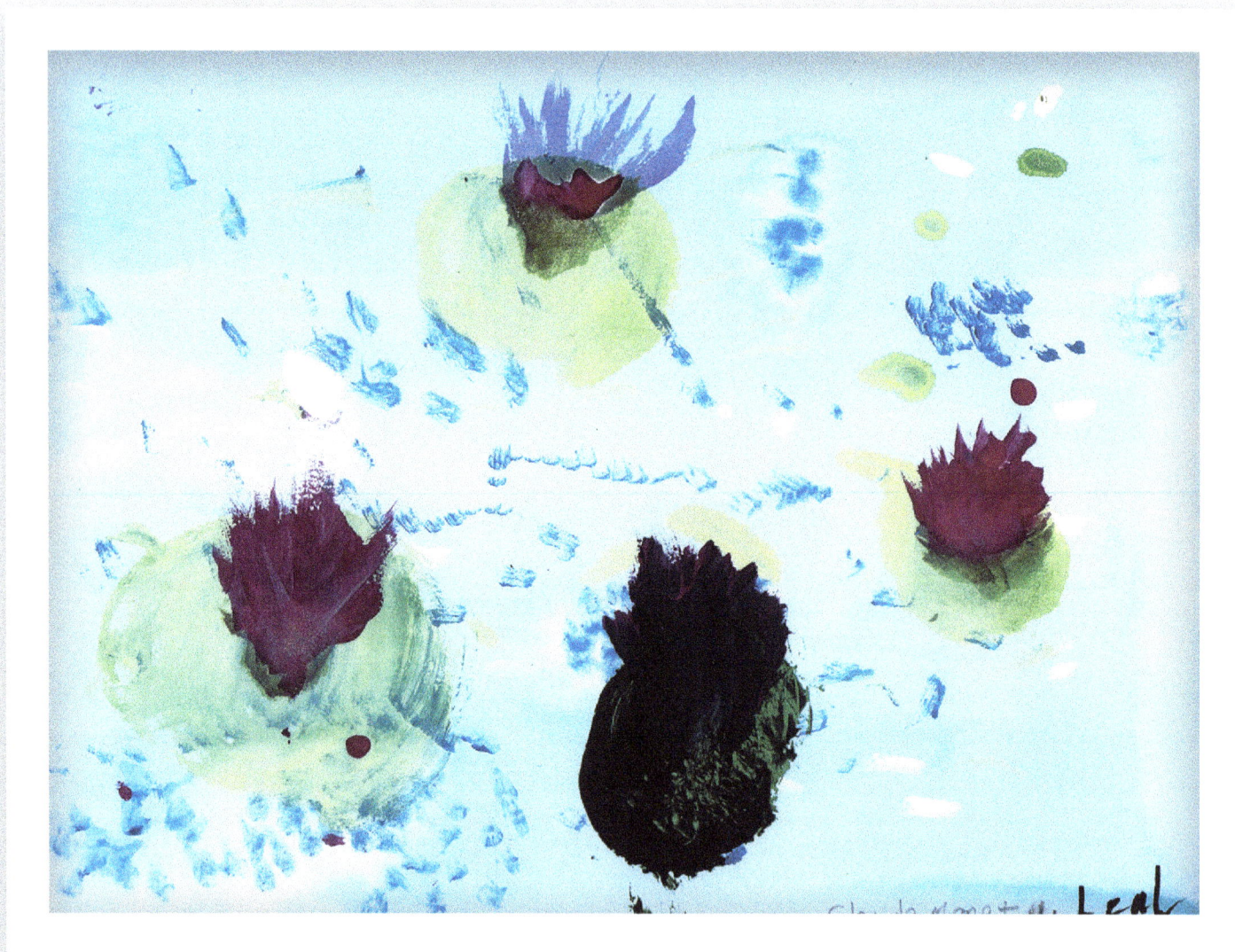

Claude Monet

Leah's Art

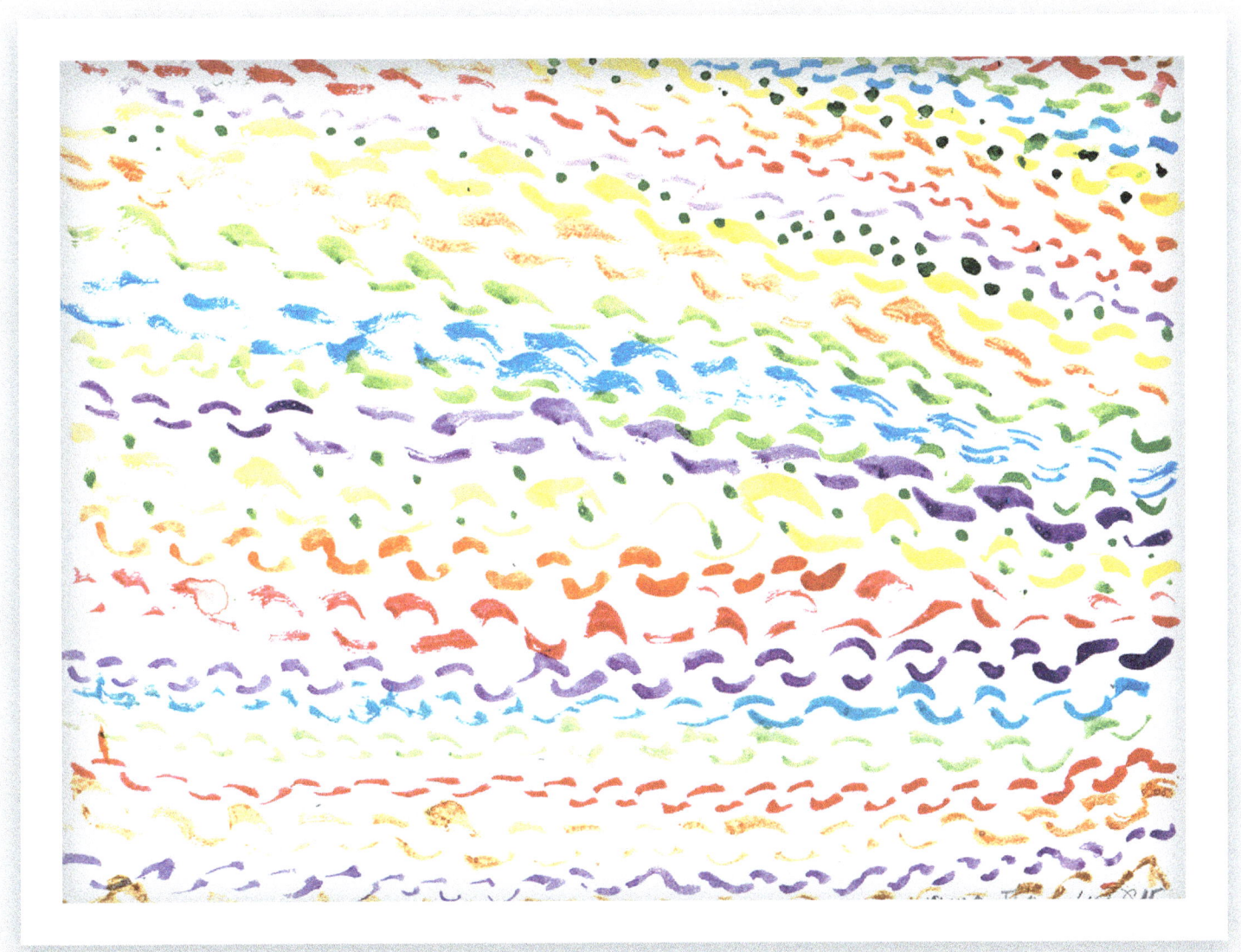

Emma Thomas

Leah Angelina Goldsmith

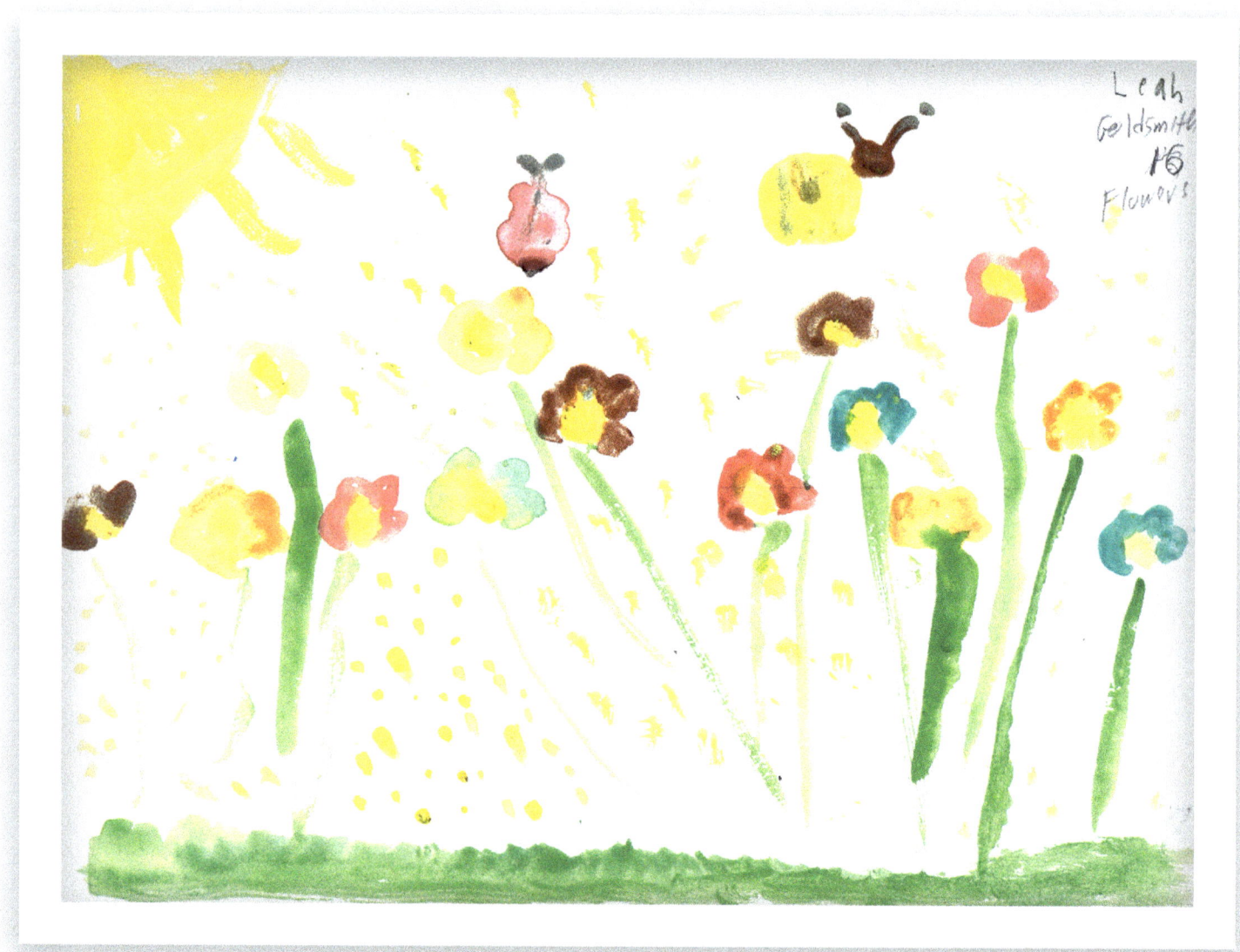

Flowers

Leah's Art

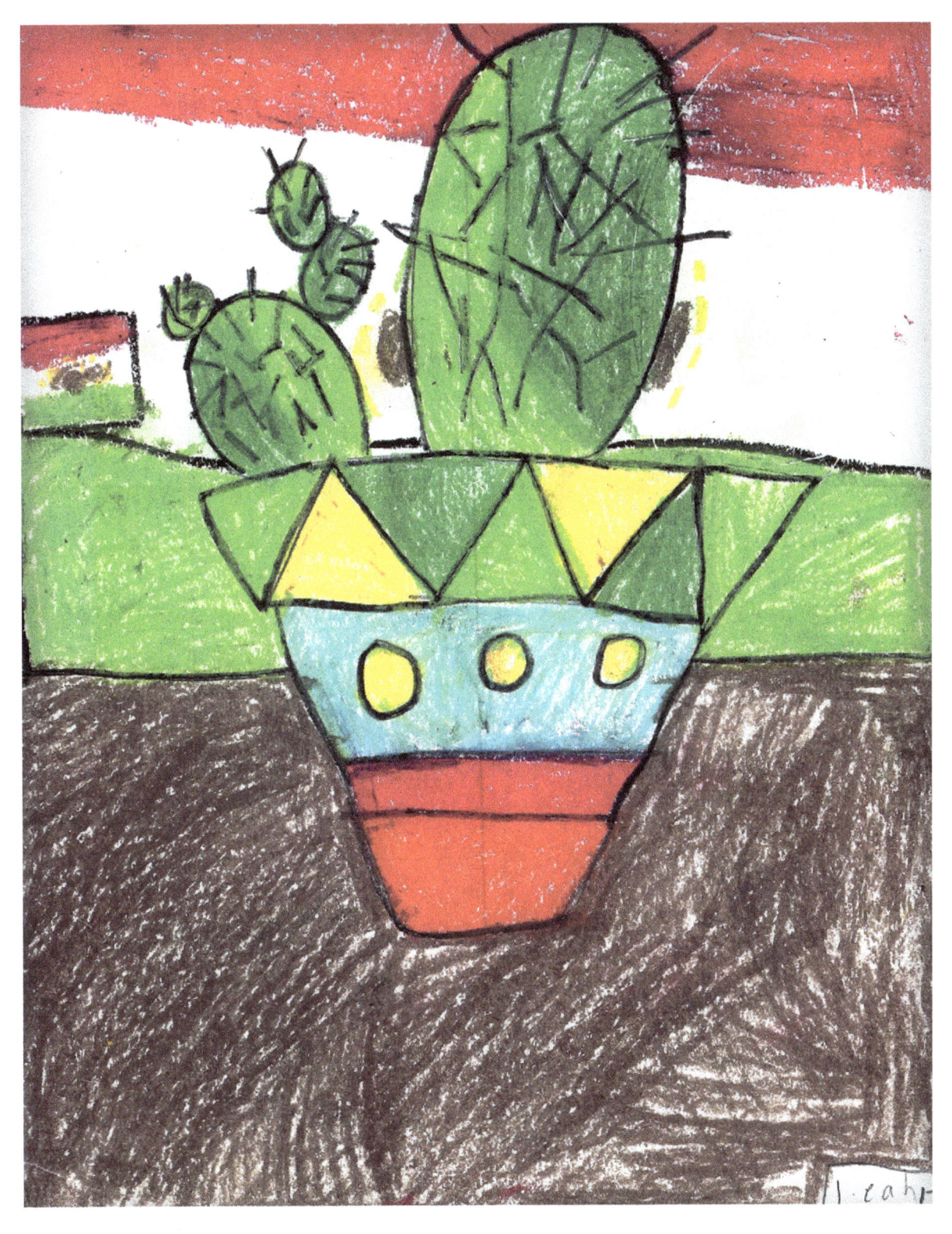

Cactus

Leah Angelina Goldsmith

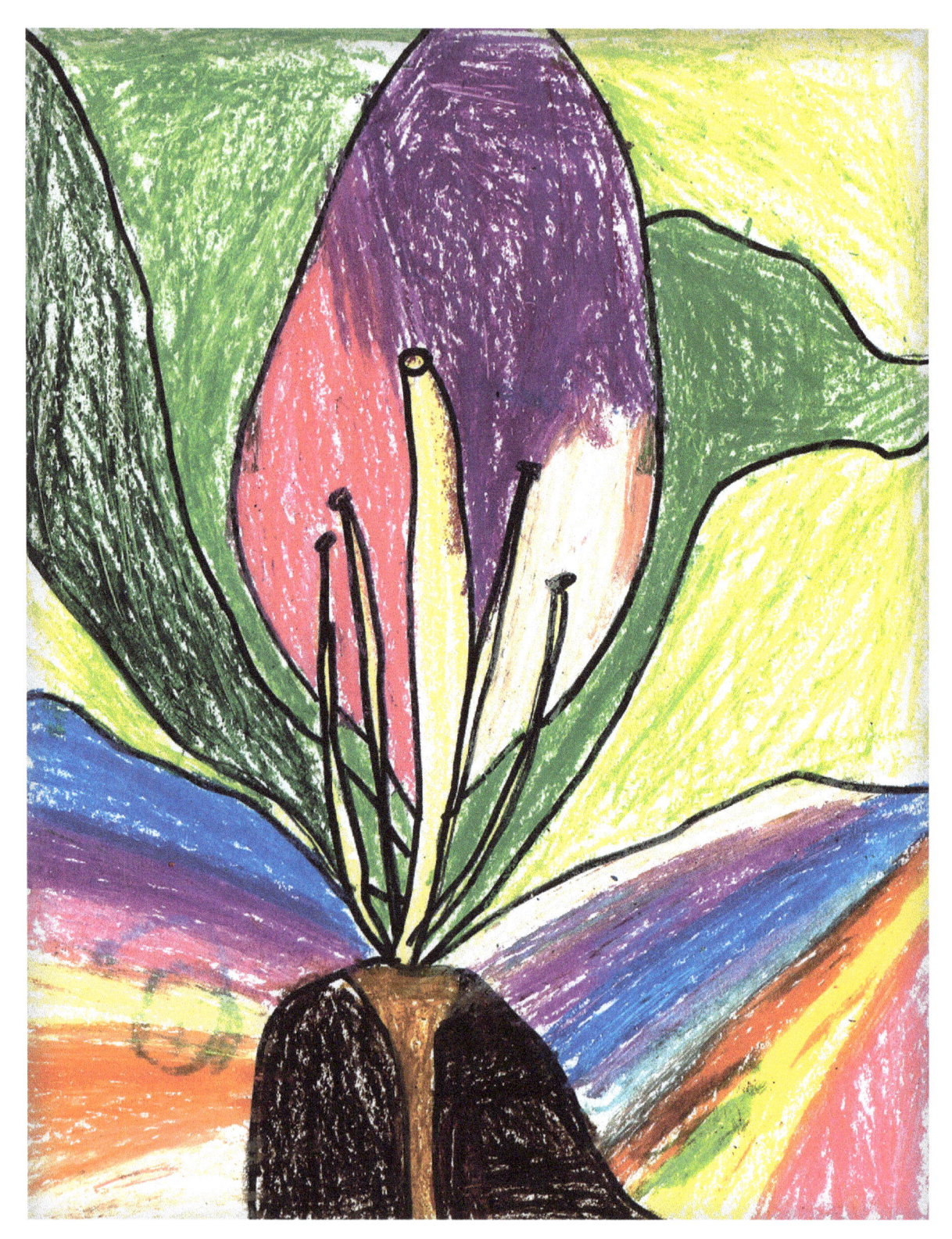

Georgia O'Keefe

Leah's Art

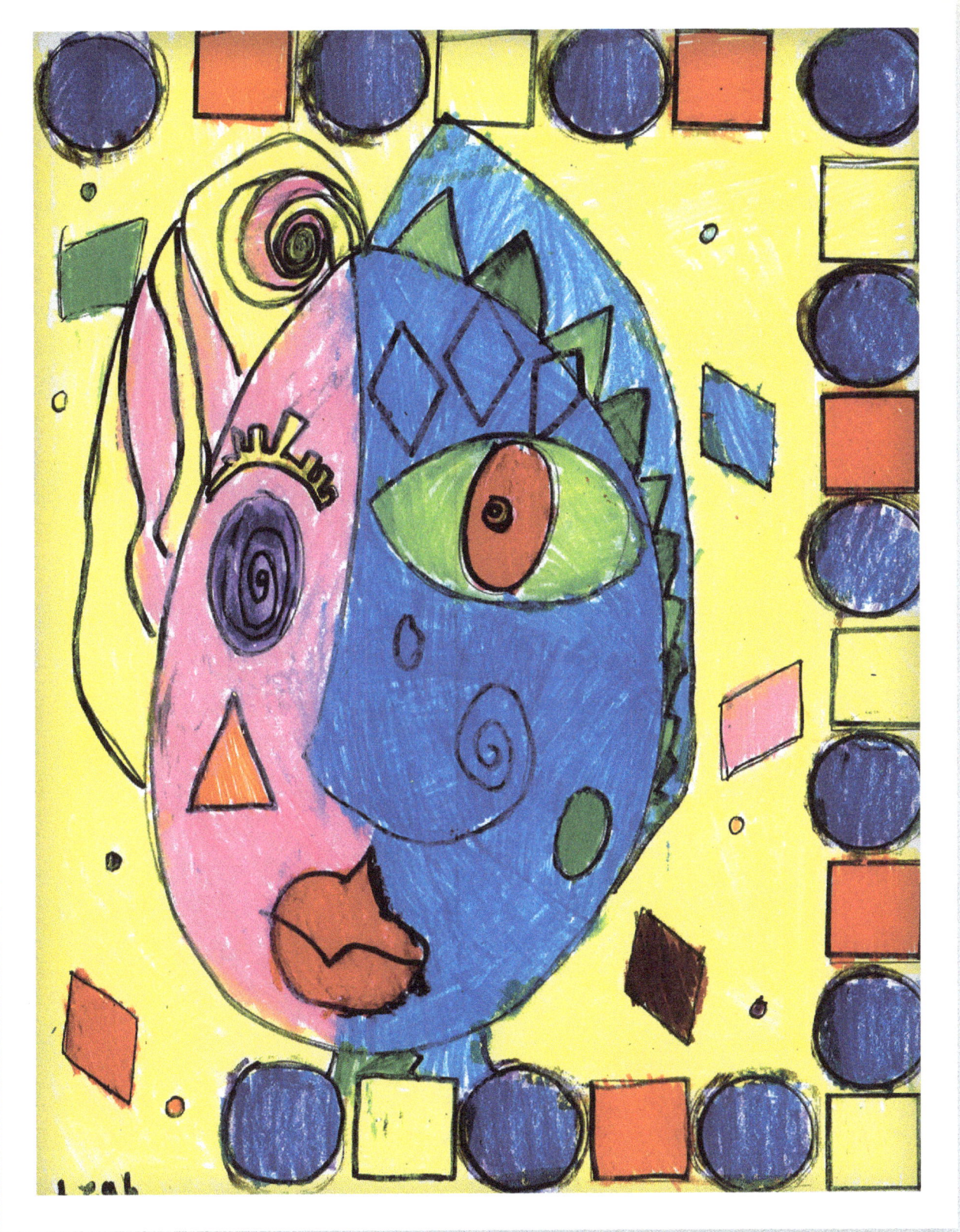

Pablo Picasso

Leah Angelina Goldsmith

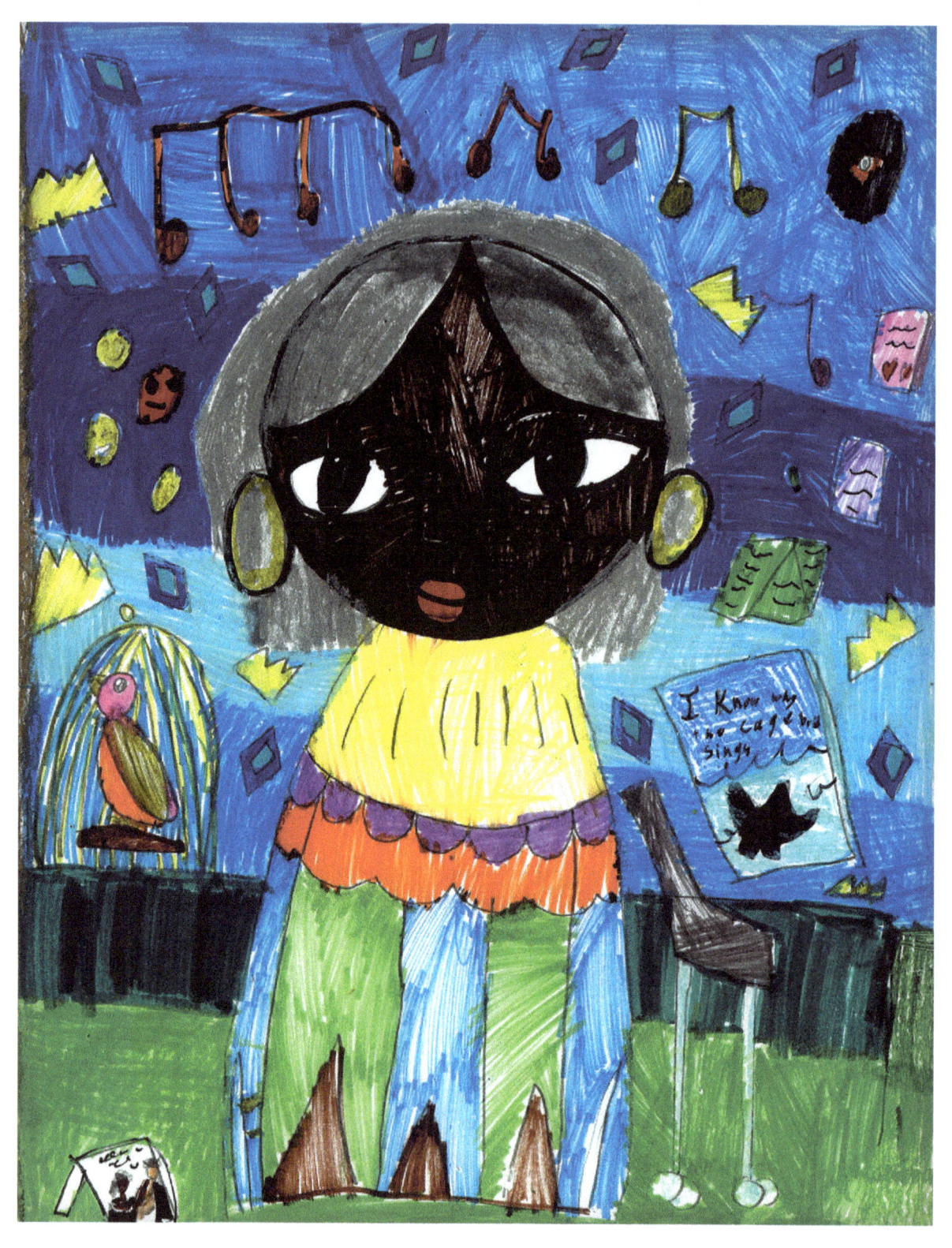

Maya Angelou

Leah's Art

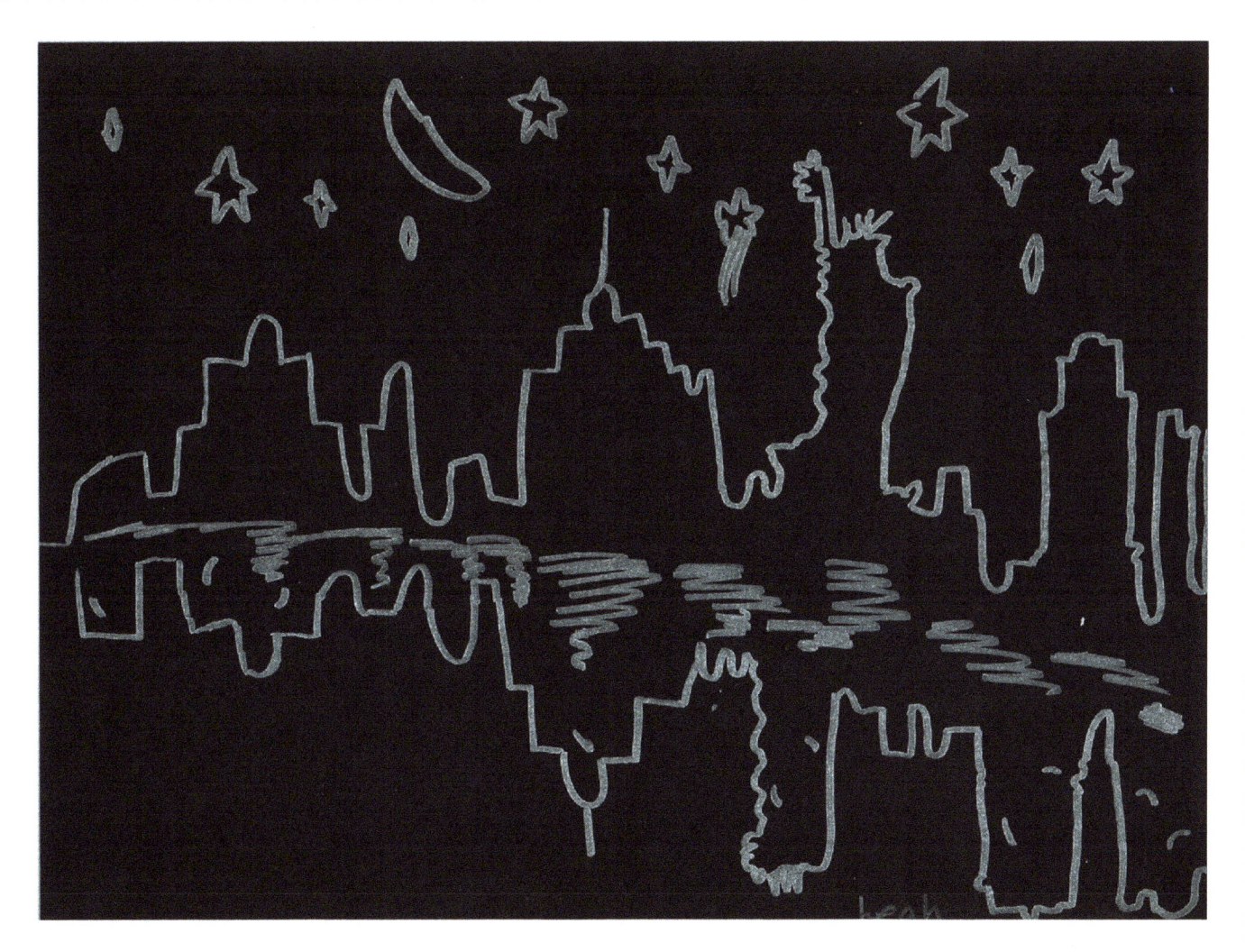

New York City, Statue of Liberty

Leah Angelina Goldsmith

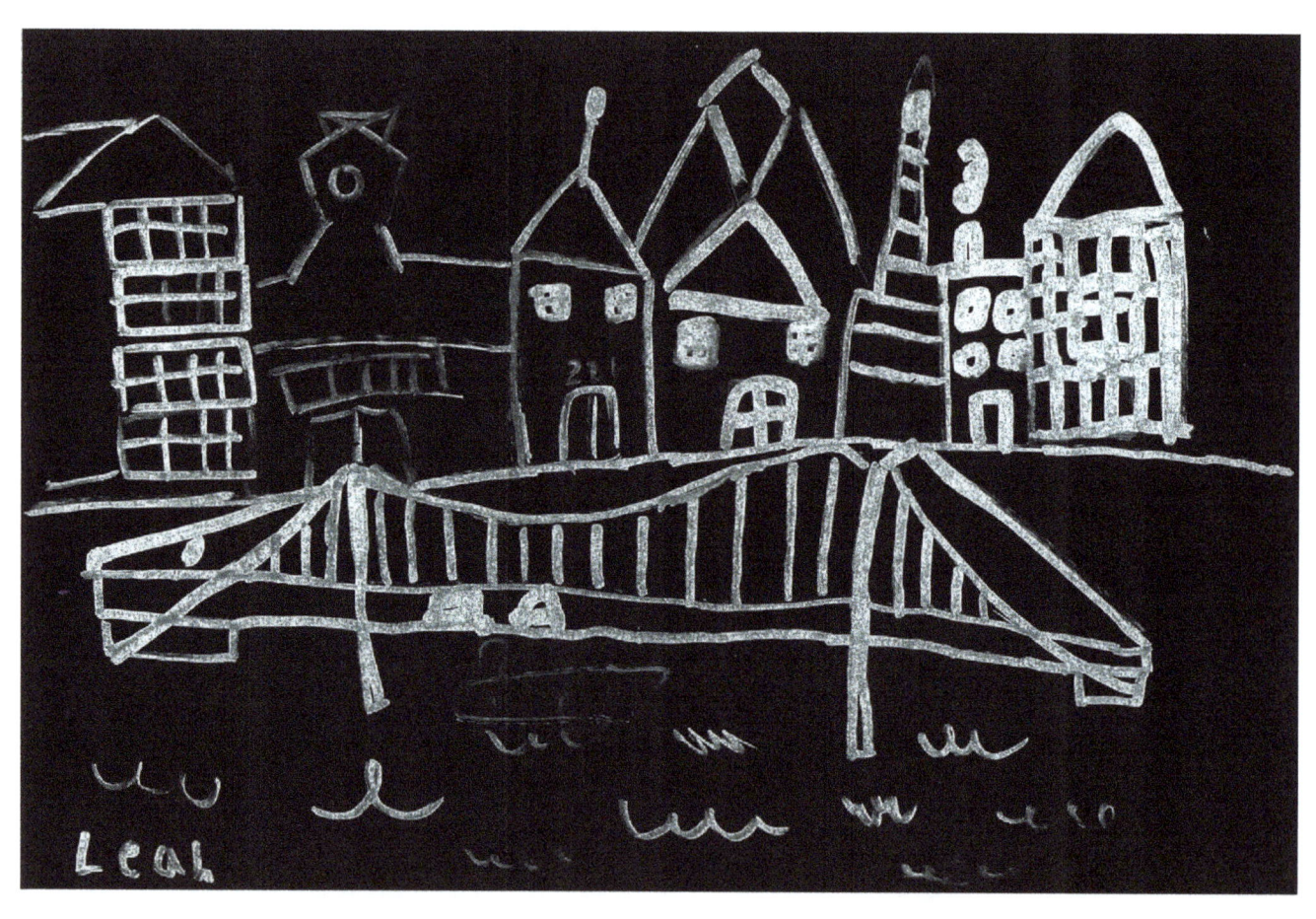

George Washington Bridge

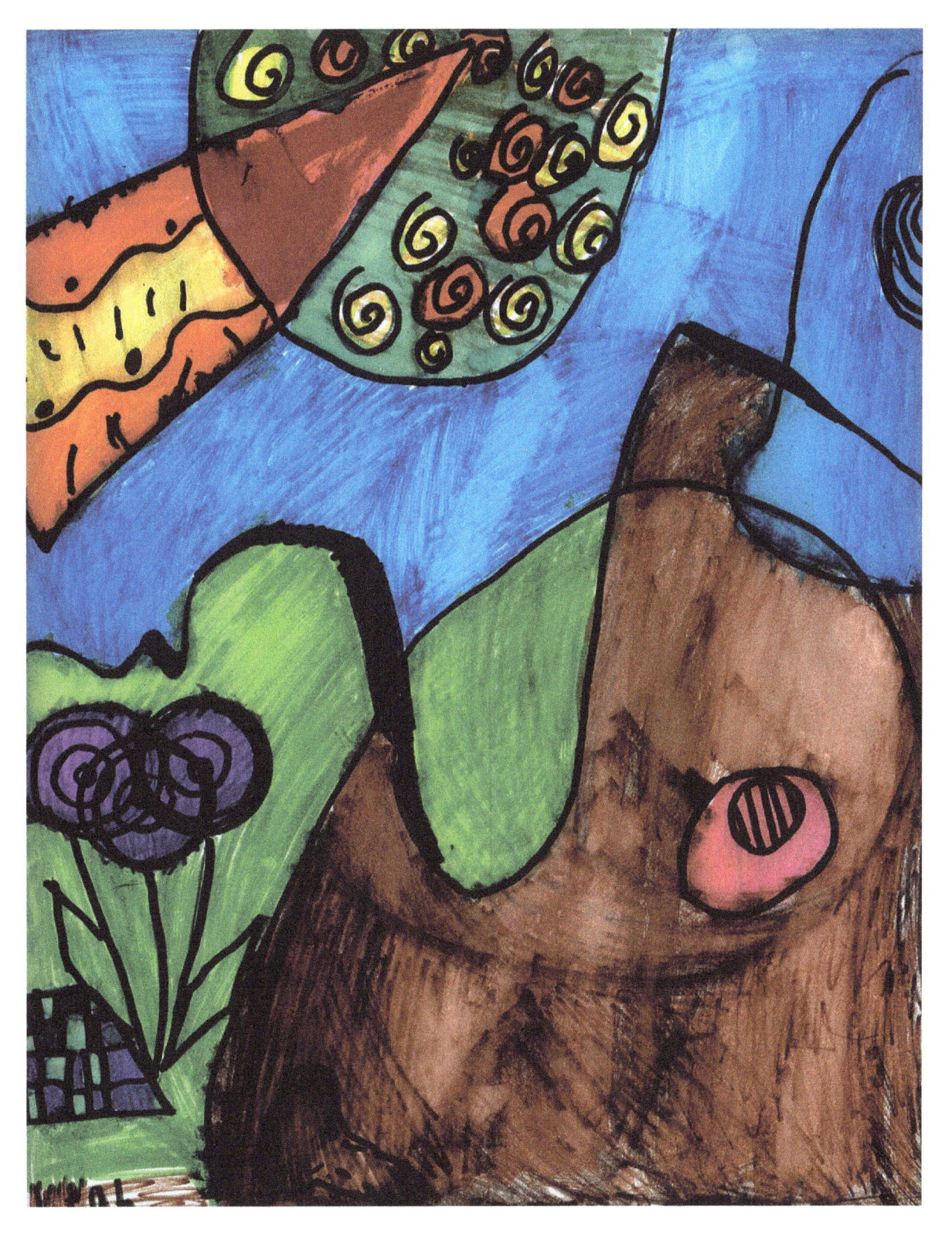

Wassily Kandinsky

Leah Angelina Goldsmith

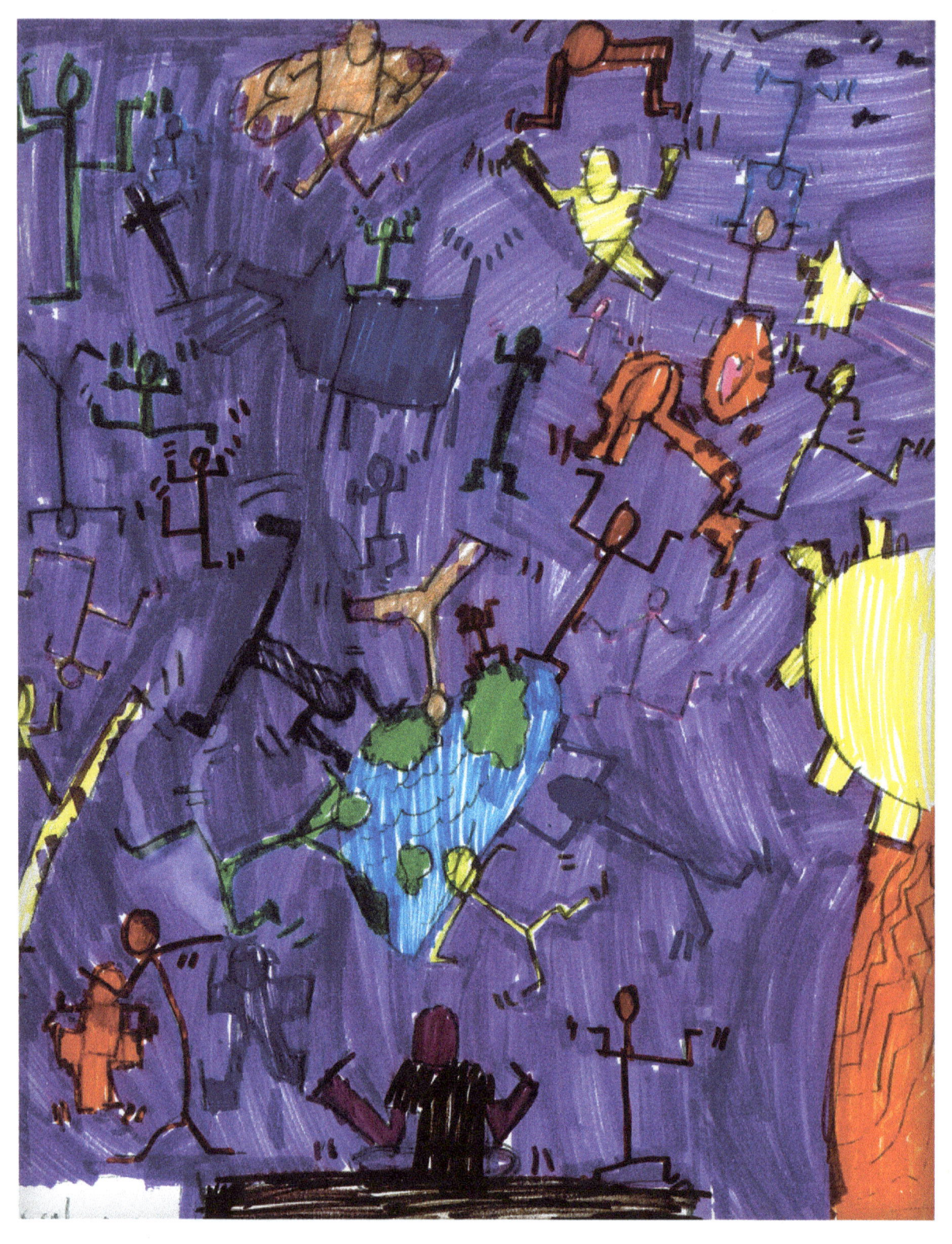

Keith Harring

About the Author

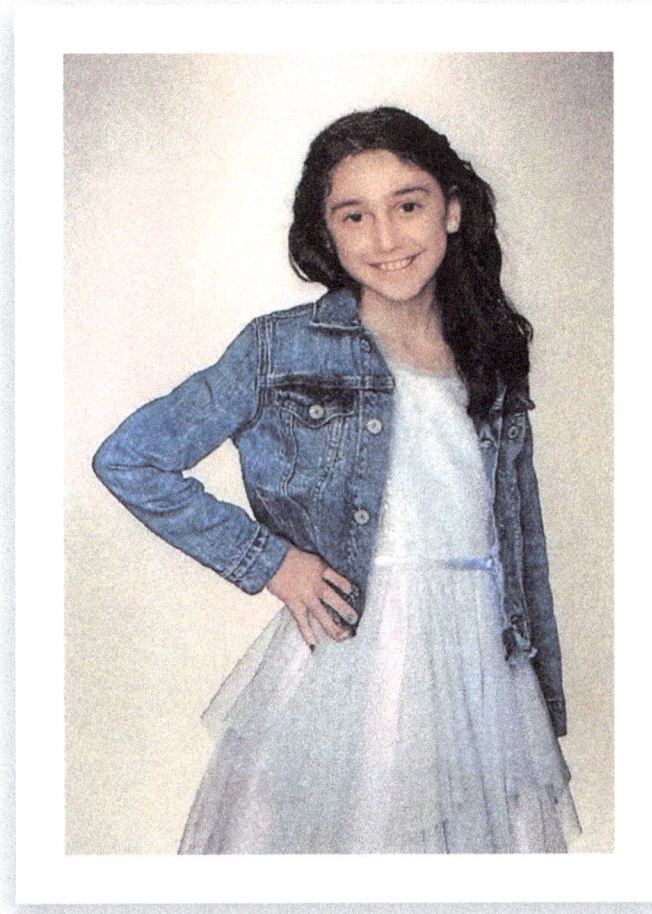

I am an 8-year-old who lives in Manhattan near Lincoln Center, surrounded by lots of culture.

In 2023-2024, I attended more than ten Broadway shows. My favorite shows were *Back to the Future, Lion King, Six, MJ, Once Upon a Mattress, New York New York, Shucked and Aladdin*. I also enjoyed seeing several wonderful dance performances at Lincoln Center – *The Nutcracker, All Balanchine, and Whipped Cream*. This year I look forward to my grandmother taking me to see my first opera and I hope to attend a music recital at Carnegie Hall.

I've been to several museums, but the Metropolitan Museum of Art was where I saw works by some of the famous artists who I learned about in school – Frida Kahlo, Andy Warhol, Henri Matisse, Claude Monet, Pablo Picasso, Jean-Michel Basquiat, and Vincent Van Gogh. Their works served as the source of inspiration for the pictures in this book. I hope my book introduces other young people to these masterpieces and inspires them to go to museums to see artworks in person.